AAT

Business Awareness

Pocket Notes

These Pocket Notes support study for the following AAT qualifications:

AAT Diploma in Accounting – Level 3

AAT Certificate in Bookkeeping – Level 3

AAT Diploma in Accounting at SCQF Level 6

British library cataloguing-in-publication data

A catalogue record for this book is available from the British Library.

Published by:
Kaplan Publishing UK
Unit 2 The Business Centre
Molly Millars Lane
Wokingham
Berkshire
RG41 2QZ

ISBN 978-1-83996-601-9

© Kaplan Financial Limited, 2023

Printed and bound in Great Britain.

CONTENTS

		Reference to Study Text chapter	Page Number

A guide to the assessment			1
Chapter 1	The business organisation	1	5
Chapter 2	The legal framework for companies and partnerships	2	15
Chapter 3	Business stakeholders' interactions and needs	3	23
Chapter 4	Organisational structure and governance	4	31
Chapter 5	The role of the finance function	5	43
Chapter 6	Risk and risk management	6	51
Chapter 7	External analysis – the PESTLE model	7	59
Chapter 8	The micro-economic environment	8	61
Chapter 9	Sustainability	8	69
Chapter 10	Professional ethics in accounting and business	8	75
Chapter 11	Money laundering	8	81
Chapter 12	Technology affecting business and finance	8	89
Chapter 13	Data protection, information security and cybersecurity	8	99

Chapter 14 Information and Big Data 8 103

Chapter 15 Visualising information 8 107

Index I.1

Preface

These Pocket Notes contain the key things that you need to know for the exam, presented in a unique visual way that makes revision easy and effective.

Written by experienced lecturers and authors, these Pocket Notes break down content into manageable chunks to maximise your concentration.

Quality and accuracy are of the utmost importance to us so if you spot an error in any of our products, please send an email to mykaplanreporting@kaplan.com with full details, or follow the link to the feedback form in MyKaplan.

Our Quality Co-ordinator will work with our technical team to verify the error and take action to ensure it is corrected in future editions.

A guide to the assessment

The assessment

BUAW is the business awareness unit on the Diploma in Accounting qualification.

Examination

Business Awareness is assessed by means of a computer-based assessment. The CBA will last for 2 hours 30 minutes and consist of 7 tasks. Some tasks will require extended (human-marked) responses.

In any one assessment, students may not be assessed on all content, or on the full depth or breadth of a piece of content. The content assessed may change over time to ensure validity of assessment, but all assessment criteria will be tested over time.

Learning outcomes & weighting

1. Understand business types, structures and governance, and the legal framework in which they operate — 25%

2. Understand the impact of the external and internal environment on businesses, their performance and decisions — 20%

3. Understand how businesses and accountants comply with principles of professional ethics — 20%

4. Understand the impact of new technologies in accounting and the risks associated with data security — 15%

5. Communicate information to stakeholders — 20%

Total — 100%

Pass mark

To pass a unit assessment, students need to achieve a mark of 70% or more.

This unit contributes 15% of the total amount required for the Diploma in Accounting qualification.

1

The business organisation

- The need for organisation and its types.
- Not for profit organisations.
- Services vs. manufacturing organisations.
- Separation of ownership and control.
- Types of funding.
- Equity and debt.

The need for organisation and its types

Organisations are social arrangements for the controlled performance of collective goals

Two or more people working together in a structured way Duties and responsibilities being assigned to each individual

Organisations use systems (e.g. swiping in when entering office) and procedures (e.g. cash handling rules) to regulate staff behaviour

All organisations pursue certain goals, these are considered to be over and above individual aspirations

Organisations exist:

- to satisfy social needs
- to overcome the individuals' limitations
- to enable individuals to specialise
- to save time through joint effort
- to pool knowledge and ideas
- to pool expertise
- to provide synergy.

Organisational types

Organisations can differ depending on their areas of activity, geographical spread of operations, size etc. However the two main types of the organisation can be classified:

1   by profit orientation

profit-seeking organisations:
seek to maximise the wealth of their owners
(e.g. commercial companies)

not-for-profit organisations (NFPs):
seek to satisfy the needs of their members, profit is no longer a primary objective (e.g. schools, hospitals).

2   by ownership/control

public sector:
provision of basic governmental services
(e.g. police, education, healthcare)

private sector limited liability (Ltds and plcs)

- partnerships
- clubs
- cooperatives owned by people who buy or use their services.

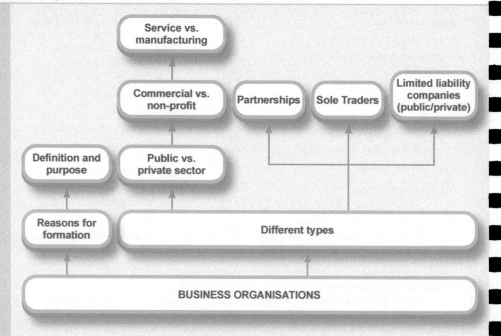

Not for profit organisations

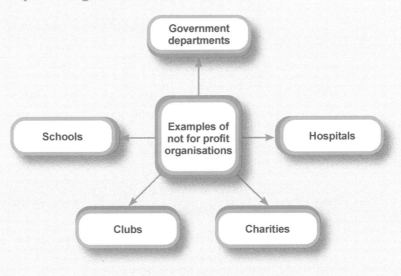

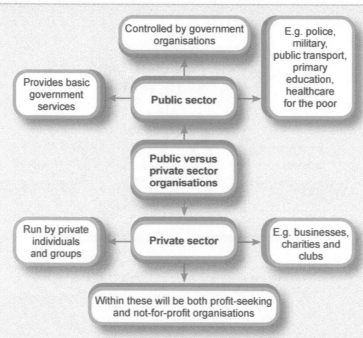

Services vs. manufacturing organisations

Differences can be remembered using the SHIP mnemonic

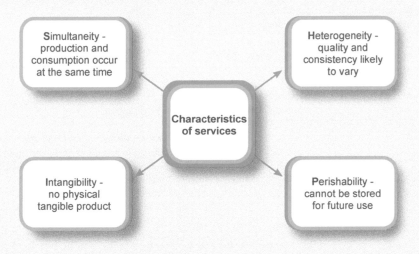

Simultaneity - production and consumption occur at the same time

Heterogeneity - quality and consistency likely to vary

Characteristics of services

Intangibility - no physical tangible product

Perishability - cannot be stored for future use

Separation of ownership and control

Reasons for separation	Benefits of separation
Specialist management expertise	Managers can concentrate on the business
Access to more capital	Shareholders earn a return on investment

Types of funding

- Public sector organisations will tend to raise money from the central government.

- Private sector organisations, such as companies and co-operatives, will most likely have to raise funds from their owners.

- Charities are usually funded by donations.

The organisation may need additional funding to allow it to grow and invest in new projects. It therefore may need to raise finance from external sources. The treasury and finance function will weigh up which source of finance best suits the circumstances of the business.

Equity and debt

Debt

This involves borrowing cash from a third party and promising to repay them at a later date. Normally the company will also have to pay interest on the amount borrowed.

Advantages:

- interest payments allowable against tax
- does not change ownership of the organisation
- tends to be cheaper to service than equity as it is often secured against assets of the company and take priority over equity in the event of the business being liquidated.

Equity

This involves selling a stake in the business in order to raise cash.

Advantages:

- no minimum level of dividend that must be paid to shareholders. Interest payments on debt finance must be paid each year
- a bank will normally require security on the company's assets before it will offer a loan. Some companies may lack quality assets to offer, making equity more attractive as it does not require security.

The legal framework for companies and partnerships

- Not for profit organisations.
- Directors.
- Shareholders.
- Unlimited liability partnerships.

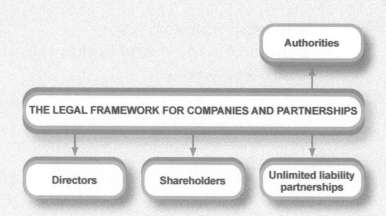

Not for profit organisations

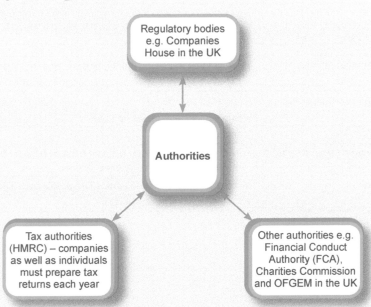

Directors

The term 'director' includes every person occupying the position or fulfilling the role of director: Every company must have at least one director and a public company must have at least two directors.

Executive director	• Likely to be a full-time employee involved in management.
	• Usually has a specific role, e.g. marketing director.
Non-executive director	• Usually part-time.
	• Brings outside expertise to board.
	• Not an employee.
Managing director ('MD')	• The board usually delegates to the MD the day-to-day management of the company's business.
Chair	• Responsible for ensuring procedure in meetings is followed.
	• Usually a non-executive director.

Directors duties

- To promote the success of the company.
- To act within powers.
- To exercise independent judgment.
- To exercise reasonable care and diligence.
- To avoid conflicts of interest.
- Not to accept benefits from third parties.
- To declare an interest in a proposed transaction or arrangement.
- To approve the financial statements and ensure that they show a true and fair view.

Shareholders

The shareholders have the right:

- To be sent a copy of annual accounts and reports.
- To require the directors to call a general meeting, and to attend general meetings.
- To receive dividends.
- To inspect company information.
- To vote on certain company affairs – subject to their class of shares and the articles of association.
- To be issued with a share certificate within two months of their shares being allotted.
- To inspect directors' service contracts.

Unlimited liability partnerships

Definition

A partnership describes 'the relationship that subsists between persons carrying on a business in common with a view to profit'.

A partnership is not a separate legal entity, and each partner has full personal liability for the partnership debts (liabilities).

When joint owners of a business are mutually responsible for the company's debt and liabilities and their personal liability isn't capped, this is known as an unlimited liability partnership.

An unlimited liability partnership, also known as a general partnership, is the default form of partnership. A partnership is often referred to as a firm.

- Partners all have unlimited personal liability: they are fully liable for any business debts. Third parties sue the partners, not the partnership as this is not a separate legal entity. The partners' liability is referred to as 'joint and several'. A third party can sue all the partners jointly, or can sue one partner individually.

- Owners may choose to trade as an unlimited partnership if they do not want to publicly file financial reports and annual accounts.

- Unlimited liability is suited to a business where the risk of insolvency is extremely low.

Goodwill

Goodwill is defined as 'the amount by which the fair value of the net assets of the partnership exceeds the carrying amount of the net assets'.

In simple terms, 'fair value' can be thought of as being the same as 'market value'.

- Goodwill arises due to factors such as reputation, location, market position, expertise and customer base.

- When a new partner joins a partnership they will not be entitled to any goodwill created by the old partnership. So the goodwill value at that point needs to be allocated to the old partners.

- A person joining a partnership will normally be expected to contribute capital to the partnership. A partner leaving a partnership would want to withdraw their capital (which will include any goodwill accumulated to the date of departure).

3

Business stakeholders' interactions and needs

- Stakeholders.
  - Connected.
  - Internal.
  - External.

A **stakeholder** is an individual or group who has an interest in what the organisation does, or who affects, or can be affected by, the organisation's actions.

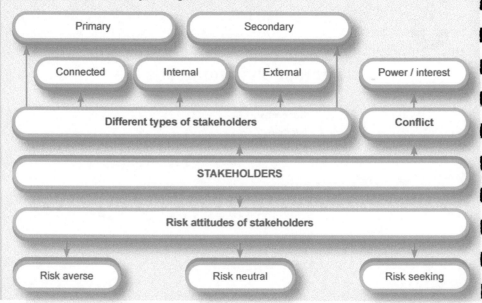

Stakeholders

There are **three categories** of stakeholder.

Internal
internal parties involved in corporate governance e.g. employees and managers

Connected
invest in, or have dealings with, the firm e.g. shareholders, customers, suppliers

External
no direct link to the firm e.g. local community, government

Each stakeholder group has different needs and expectations in relation to the organisation.

Conflicts

An organisation can have many different stakeholders, all with different needs. Inevitably, the needs of some stakeholders will come into conflict with the needs of others.

Some of the most common conflicts include:

Stakeholders	Conflict
Employees versus managers	Jobs/wages versus profit-linked bonus (improved by cost efficiency)
Customers versus shareholders	Product quality/service levels versus profits/dividends
General public versus shareholders	Effect on the environment versus profit/dividends
Managers versus shareholders	Independence versus growth

If an organisation is having difficulty deciding who the dominant stakeholder is, it can use **Mendelow's power-interest matrix**.

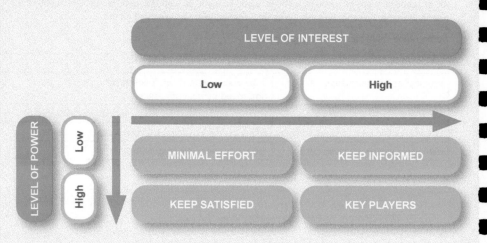

Managers need to consider the needs of as many stakeholders as possible when making decisions. This means that nearly every decision becomes a compromise.

Attitudes to risk

It is important to understand the tolerance levels of the stakeholders in relation to various factors including cost, quality, etc.

It is also important to accept that not all stakeholders will have the same attitude towards risk.

Organisational structure and governance

- Entrepreneurial.
- Functional/departmental structure.
- Divisional/product structure.
- Divisions based on geographical areas.
- Matrix structure.
- Tall and flat organisations.
- Governance.
- Planning levels.
- Governance and structure.

Entrepreneurial

This structure is built around the owner manager and is typical of small businesses in the early stages of development.

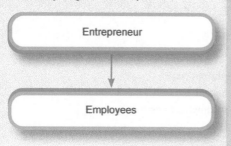

Advantages

- Fast decision making
- More responsive to market
- Goal congruence
- Good control
- Close bond to workforce

Disadvantages

- Lack of career structure
- Dependent on the capabilities of the manager/owner
- Cannot cope with diversification/growth

Functional/departmental structure

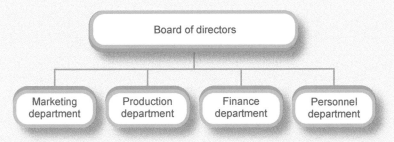

Advantages

- Economies of scale
- Standardisation
- Specialists more comfortable
- Career opportunities

Disadvantages

- Empire building
- Slow
- Conflicts between functions
- Cannot cope with diversification

Divisional/product structure

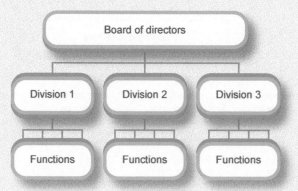

A **shared service approach** involves restructuring the provision of certain services within the organisation so that the service is centralised into one specific part of the organisation.

Divisions based on geographical areas

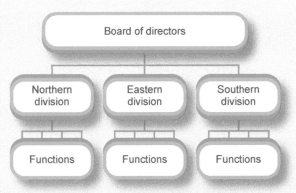

Advantages

- Enables growth
- Clear responsibility for products/ divisions
- Training of general managers
- Easily adapted for further diversification
- Top management free to concentrate on strategic matters

Disadvantages

- Potential loss of control
- Lack of goal congruence
- Duplication
- Specialists may feel isolated
- Allocation of central costs can be a problem

Matrix structure

Matrix structures are a combination of the functional and divisional structures.

Advantages

- Advantages of both functional and divisional structures
- Flexibility
- Customer orientation
- Encourages teamwork and the exchange of opinions and expertise

Disadvantages

- Dual command and conflict
- Dilution of functional authority
- Time-consuming meetings
- Higher admin costs

Tall and flat organisations

Span of control

Scalar chain is the line of authority which can be traced up or down the chain of command from the most senior member of staff to the most junior. It relates to the number of levels of management within an organisation.

A manager's **span of control** is the number of people for whom he or she is directly responsible.

Factors that influence the span of control include:

- the nature of the work – the more repetitive or simple the work, the wider the span of control can be.
- the type of personnel – the more skilled and motivated the managers and the other staff members are, the wider the span of control can be.

- the location of personnel – if personnel are all located locally, it takes relatively little time and effort to supervise them. This allows the span of control to become wider.

Tall and flat organisations

A **tall organisation** has many levels of management (a long scalar chain and a narrow span of control).

A **flat organisation** has few levels of management (a short scalar chain and a wide span of control).

Governance

Governance refers to the authority structures, processes, and rules that an organisation has in place to determine how decisions get made, resources get allocated, and priorities get set.

Governance will therefore require the organisation to make decisions on the following areas:

- Specialisation: the extent to which an organisation's activities are divided into specialised roles.
- Standardisation: the degree to which an organisation operates under standard rules or procedures.
- Formalisation: the extent to which instructions and procedures are documented.

- Centralisation: the degree to which leaders at the top of the management hierarchy have authority to make certain decisions.
- Chain of command: the number of vertical levels or layers on the organisational chart (i.e. how tall the structure should be).
- Span of control: how wide or narrow this should be.

Centralisation and decentralisation

- In a centralised structure, the upper levels of an organisation's hierarchy retain the authority and make decisions.
- In a decentralised structure, the authority to take decisions is passed down to units and people at lower levels.

The factors that will affect the amount of decentralisation are:

- management style
- ability of management/employees
- geographic spread
- size of the organisation/scale of activities
- predictability of the environment.

Advantages of decentralisation

- Senior management free to concentrate on strategy.
- Better local decisions due to local expertise.
- Better motivation due to increased training and career path.
- Quicker responses/flexibility, due to smaller chain of command.

Disadvantages of decentralisation

- Loss of control by senior management.
- Dysfunctional decisions due to a lack of goal congruence.
- Poor decisions made by inexperienced managers.
- Training costs.
- Duplication of roles within the organisation.
- Extra costs in obtaining information.

Planning levels

Strategic planning

- Information predominantly environmental. Information imprecise and speculative.
- Long-term forecasts.
- Main output targets and plans.
- Ad hoc control system.

Management control

- Information concerned with efficiency and effective use of resources in the whole organisation.
- Information in financial and volume terms.
- May involve responsibility centres.
- Includes measures of productivity, budget performance, labour and capacity utilisation.

Operational control

- Short-term control information.
- Very detailed.
- May be in terms of quantity, rates and times rather than finance.

Governance and structure

Different governance is likely to be applied to different structures.

Entrepreneurial structure		Divisional structure
Little	Specialisation	Lots
Little	Standardisation	Lots
Little	Formalisation	Lots
Very high	Centralisation	Very low
Flat	Chain of command	Tall
Wide	Span of control	Narrow

The role of the finance function

- Operations/production.
  - Sales and Marketing.
  - Human resources.
  - Finance.
  - IT.
  - Distribution and Logistics.

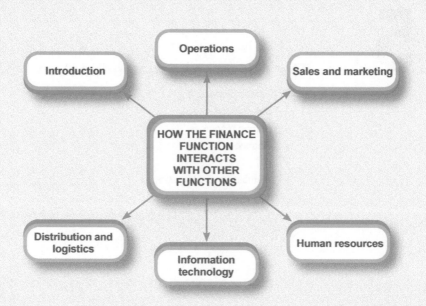

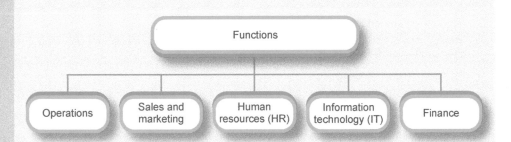

Operations/production

Interaction between production and finance

Specific parts of the organisation's operations (purchasing, production and service provision) interact with the finance function.

Purchasing (procurement)

Purchasing is responsible for placing and following up orders. It will co-ordinate with the finance function as follows:

Establishing credit terms	Finance will work with purchasing to negotiate credit terms with suppliers.
Prices	Finance will advise purchasing on the best price to pay suppliers.
Payment	Approved by purchasing and made by finance.
Data capture	Order details are input by purchasing and shared with finance.
Budgeting	Finance will consult with purchasing on the likely budget costs.

Production

The production of goods is a core part of the operations function. It liaises with the finance function as follows:

Costing	Finance will calculate production costs using information provided by operations.
Budgeting	Finance and operations will work together to determine the budgeted cost of production.
Cost v quality	Finance and operations will work together to establish the optimum balance between cost and quality.
Production process	Finance can assist in identifying inefficiencies in the production process (such as bottlenecks) and suggest improvements.
Inventory	Use various techniques to advise on stock levels and production required to meet demand.

Finance interaction with sales and marketing

The finance function will work with the sales and marketing function in the areas of:

Budgeting	Finance will discuss the likely sales volume with sales and marketing, in order to produce the sales budget.
Advertising	Finance will help set the budget and monitor the benefit generated.
Pricing	Finance will have an input into setting the optimum price.
Market share	Finance can provide sales volume information and help to determine market share.
Key Performance Indicators (KPIs)	Finance will help to establish and monitor the KPIs for sales and marketing.

Product/service development

Given the rapidly changing nature of the modern consumer's needs, effective product/service development is core to achieving or maintaining competitive advantage in the market.

With a sharp eye for the economic upside (or otherwise) the finance function will work collaboratively with sales and marketing to evaluate new product/service lines.

Interaction between HR and finance

- **Traditionally**, the HR function and the finance function worked independently. Finance viewed people as a cost whereas HR viewed them as an **asset**. Collaboration was limited, for example to establishing a budget for a reward programme.

- The **modern** approach is to view people as one of the **greatest assets** of the organisation and that finance and HR should work more closely with the 'people as assets' as their focus.

- Both functions have **overlapping responsibilities**, for example considering the costs and benefits of different HR policies.

Interaction between IT and finance

IT is one of the **greatest assets** of the organisation and that finance and IT should work more closely resulting in, for example:

- Smarter investment in IT.
- Improvements in information security and compliance.
- Improved data analytics.

SCM interaction with finance

- The role of the supply chain leader has become more prominent in recent years as the focus of SCM has moved away from cost reductions to creating a strategy that is aligned to the broader goals of the organisation.

- Meanwhile, the role of the finance function has been transformed. Finance now collaborates more closely with other functions; not just from a monitoring, reporting and risk management perspective, but also as supporters and enablers of performance.

6

Risk and risk management

- What is risk?
- Types of risk.
- Risk management.

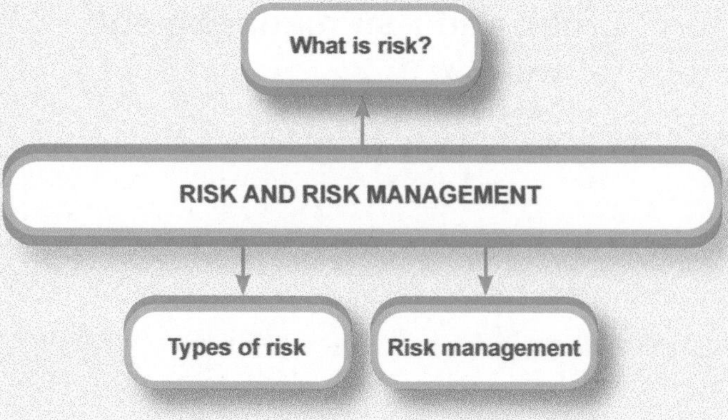
What is risk?
RISK AND RISK MANAGEMENT
Types of risk
Risk management

What is risk?

Definition

Risk, in business, is the chance that future events or results may not be as expected. Risk can be quantified by assigning probabilities to various levels of loss.

Upside risks and downside risks

- Downside risk is the risk that results may be worse than expected.
- Upside risk is the risk that results may be better than expected.

The difference between risk and uncertainty

Risk is quantifiable; possible outcomes have associated probabilities and allow the use of mathematical techniques.

Uncertainty is unquantifiable, and the outcome cannot be mathematically modelled. It is difficult to incorporate uncertainty into decision making models.

Risk and return

Reasons why companies take risks include:

- To increase financial return – It is generally the case that firms must be willing to take higher risks if they want to achieve higher returns.
- To gain competitive advantage – To generate higher returns a business may have to take more risk in order to be competitive. Conversely, not accepting risk tends to make a business less dynamic and implies a 'follow the leader' strategy.

Investors may have different risk appetites. Some investors may be willing to take high risks whilst others prefer to seek only low risk opportunities. These different attitudes should be accepted and tolerated, and should not be the cause of prejudicial or discriminatory behaviour.

Types of risk

Business risk

This is the risk that the business fails. There are many sources of business risk such as:

- Strategic risk – the risk that the organisation's strategy (such as a strategy to enter a new overseas market) fails.

- Environmental risk – the risk that the organisation fails to adapt to changes in its environment (such as failing to adapt to new technology or new regulations).

- Product risk – the risk that the organisation's products fail (such as new products do not sell well or customers stop buying existing products).

- Market risk – the risk that the organisation fails to adapt to changes in its market (such as failing to react to new innovations by rivals or new rivals entering the market).

Operational risk

> **Definition**

Operational risk refers to potential losses that might arise in business operations. It is 'the risk of losses resulting from inadequate or failed internal processes, people and systems, or external events' (Basel Committee on Banking Supervision).

Examples of operational risk are:

- Business disruption risk – this is the risk that the organisation's operations cannot continue to operate as normal.

- Regulatory risk – this is the risk that the business fails to meet regulatory standards or legislation.

- People risk – this is the risk of errors or problems caused by the people within the organisation.

- Process risk – this is the risk that processes are not efficient or fail.

Cyber risk

Definition

Cyber risk is a type of operational risk and is the risk of financial loss, disruption, or damage to an organisation caused by issues with the information technology systems they use.

- Malware – this is a term used to describe different types of malicious software, regardless of the purpose.
- Ransomware – software that prevents access to data until a ransom is paid.
- Botnets – networks of infected computers that are under the control of an attacker.
- Spyware – malware that is designed to spy on the victim and report back to the attacker.
- Trojans – legitimate software that secretly contains and releases malicious software onto a system.

- Malvertising – online advertising that has malicious software written into its code.
- Viruses – malware that replicates itself and spreads through programs, files and data.

Reputational risk

Definition

Reputation is the opinions people have and communicate about something, so reputational risk is the risk that people will have a negative opinion of an organisation and share that opinion with other people.

Reputation risk is for many organisations a down-side risk as the better the reputation of the business the more risk there is of losing that reputation.

There is a variety of considerations:

- Employees – the actions and behaviour of staff reflect the principles of the organisation they work for.

- Management – their position implies they are more likely to reflect the core values of the business, any digression is more significant.

- Accounting – any company found to be operating dubious accounting practices would lose confidence of customers and investors.

- Fraud – if a company allows fraud to take place, or does not allow appropriate action, it can lead to concerns from stakeholders.

- Bribery and corruption – if an organisation acts in an appropriate manner by offering or accepting bribery or any form of corruption this will damage their reputation.

Financial risk

Definition

Financial risk is the risk of change in a financial condition such as an exchange rate, interest rate, credit rating of a customer, or the price of goods.

Financial risks can come from a number of areas:

- Credit risk – the risk of non-payment by customers.

- Interest rate risk – the risk that interest rates change.

- Debt risk (gearing risk) – the risk that high levels of debt increase the risk of the business being bankrupt.

Risk management

The TARA framework

- Transfer – transfer risk wholly or in part to a third party e.g. by taking out insurance.

- Avoid – many risks are unavoidable, so the only choice here may be not to invest.

- Reduce – reduce or mitigate risks by limiting probability and/or impact, especially of downside exposure.

- Accept – accept the risk and deal with the consequences.

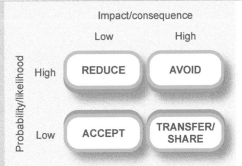

External analysis
– the PESTLE model

- – Political.
- – Economic.
- – Social.
- – Technological.
- – Legal.
- – Environmental.

Political factors	Economic factors	Social factors
• Taxation policy • Government spending • Foreign trade	• Economic growth • Exchange/interest rates • Inflation	• Attitudes • Demographics • Income distribution

EXTERNAL ANALYSIS – THE PESTLE MODEL
PESTLE Analysis of the macro environment

Technological factors	Legal factors	Environmental / ecological factors
• New products • Production methods • Obsolescence	• Industry regulation • Competition legislation • Employment law	• Sustainability • Climate change • Natural capital impact

8

The micro-economic environment

- Microeconomics.
- Demand.
- Supply.
- The price mechanism.
- Competition.

Microeconomics

Part of an organisation's external PESTLE analysis will involve assessing the economic factors which will affect its industry. The key issue is to identify potential opportunities and threats.

Economics can be defined in various ways, including:

'the study of how society allocates scarce resources which have alternative uses, between competing ends'

It is useful to distinguish between two aspects of economics:

Microeconomics – the study of the economic behaviour of individual consumers, firms and industries.

Macroeconomics – considers aggregate behaviour, and the study of the sum of individual economic decisions – in other words, the workings of the economy as a whole.

Demand

Individual and market demand

Individual demand represents the amount that a consumer is willing and able to purchase at a given price – i.e. effective demand. Market demand shows the total amount of effective demand from all the consumers in a market.

Factors that shift the demand curve:

prices of other goods	Substitutes v complementary goods
income	Compare normal goods v inferior goods
taste/fashion	Could be influenced by advertising
other factors	Population size, credit terms

Changes in the price of the good/service do not shift the demand curve, they lead to an **expansion** or **contraction** along the curve.

This may be due to the **income effect** (as goods become more expensive, consumers can buy less of them), or the **substitution effect** (as goods become more expensive, consumers opt for cheaper alternatives)

As the price of a good rises, we expect demand for a normal good to fall, hence why the demand curve slopes **downwards**.

Supply

Supply is the amount that producers are willing and able to produce at a given price.

Factors that shift the supply curve

prices of other goods	Better to make them instead?
cost changes	e.g. new technology, greater efficiency, greater productivity, change in indirect taxes, e.g. VAT

Changes in the price of the good/service do not shift the supply curve, they lead to an **expansion** or **contraction** along the curve.

As the price of a good rises, we expect supply to rise, as suppliers are willing and able to produce more of it (due to the higher profits), hence why the supply curve slopes **upwards**.

The price mechanism

Equilibrium price set by the interaction of supply and demand

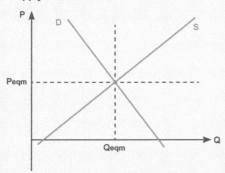

Price higher than equilibrium	Price lower than equilibrium
Excess supply – producers drop prices to clear surplus	Excess demand – shortages force prices up

Shifts in supply/demand

- Changes in supply/demand result in new equilibrium price.

- In exam questions consider whether it is the supply curve or the demand curve that is moving and in which direction.

- Example - for supply and demand of tea bags, a good tea harvest will reduce the cost of the tea leaves, making it cheaper to supply the product so the supply curve shifts outwards (S1 to S2). This increases the quantity sold to Q2 at a reduced price of P2.

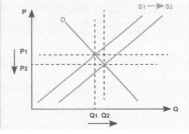

Competition

Healthy competition in a market benefits consumers. If competition is strong, with suppliers vying for the attention of customers, product / service quality will tend to rise and prices will be reasonable.

In this section, we look at various factors that determine the levels of competition for microeconomic markets.

Product features

Competition will be higher among products that are undifferentiated from their competitors' products. Those that are differentiated will have something about them that stands out and attracts customers that other products do not.

The more unique a product is, the more differentiated it will be and the fewer direct competitors it will have.

Number of sellers and buyers

Examples of markets where competition will be reduced are:

- Monopoly. One company controls all or nearly all of the market for a particular product or service and no major competitors.
- Monopolistic competition. A business has many different competitors, but each offers a somewhat differentiated product.
- Oligopoly. The market is controlled by a small number of organisations.

Barriers to entry

Barriers to entry are factors that make it difficult for a new entrant to gain an initial foothold in a market.

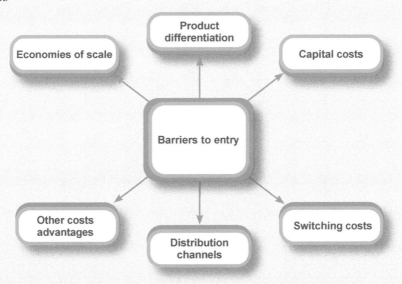

9

Sustainability

- Benefits of acting sustainably.
- Sustainability and corporate social responsibility (CSR).
- Triple bottom line reporting (TBL).

Benefits of acting sustainably

Acting sustainably can contribute to the long-term success of the business and will help to maintain the well-being of the planet and people.

Benefits to stakeholders of the organisation include:

Stakeholder	Benefit
Workers/local community	Reduced waste and pollution will lead to a more pleasant, healthier environment. Guarantee of an appropriate minimum wage will lead to a better standard of living. Better workplace conditions will attract a higher calibre of workers and reduce accidents / injuries.
Customers	Many customers prefer dealing with businesses that follow sustainable policies such as looking after the environment or providing good working conditions and opportunities for workers, as they are seen as being more ethical.
Supply chain	Integrating sustainability into the supply chain will help suppliers achieve their own sustainability goals.
Shareholders	Shareholders look for an economically sound investment. Reduction of waste and increased efficiency can improve business profits. This could lead to higher long-term returns for investors.
Public	Businesses that are economically sound provide a stable job market for workers. Reduced pollution can lead to fewer environmental problems.

Three aspects of sustainable performance

It is important to note that sustainability is more than just looking at environmental concerns. It relates to three aspects:

- Environmental (planet).
- Social (people).
- Economic (profit) aspects of human society.

Some examples of unsustainable practices are:

Economic

- Underpayment of taxes – not contributing to maintaining the country's infrastructure (schools, roads, etc.).
- Bribery and corruption.

Social

- Rich companies exploiting third world labour as cheap manufacturing.

Environmental

- Long term damage to the environment from carbon dioxide and other greenhouse gases.

A key challenge is to ensure that organisations remain profitable while improving their environmental and social performance.

Sustainability affects every level of life, from the local neighbourhood to the entire planet.

> It is ethically wrong for this generation to benefit at the expense of future generations.

Sustainability and corporate social responsibility (CSR)

'CSR is the continuing commitment by business to behave ethically and contribute to economic development while improving the quality of life of the workforce and their families as well as of the local community and society at large.' (WBCSD meeting in The Netherlands, 1998).

Sustainability is thus one aspect of corporate social responsibility (CSR) and the two concepts are closely linked.

This is significant because many companies already have a commitment to CSR, setting targets and producing reports, for example. Calls for greater sustainability can thus be seen in the context of developing a firm's existing CSR policies and responsibilities, rather than something different and new.

Triple bottom line reporting (TBL)

- TBL accounting expands the traditional company reporting framework to take into account environmental and social performance in addition to financial/economic performance.
- Looks at reporting performance and decision making.
- The concept is also explained using the triple 'P' headings of 'People, Planet and Profit'.

Having a TBL perspective

A TBL business would attempt to do the following:

People

- Pay its workers fair wages.
- Maintain a safe working environment.
- Not use child labour or use suppliers who do.

Chapter 9

- Promote the communities in which it operates.

Planet

- Reduce its 'ecological footprint'.
- Reduce energy usage.
- Limit environmental damage.
- Not be involved in resource depletion.

Profit

- Try to balance the profit objective with the other two elements of the TBL.

TBL thus attempts to show the full cost of any plans or development.

Once targets are set for these aspects and performance measured, then firms will incorporate the effects into decision making ('what gets measured gets done').

10

Professional ethics in accounting and business

- Fundamental Principles (IFAC Code of Ethics).
- Threats.
- Safeguards.

Definition

Ethics can be defined as the 'moral principles that govern a person's behaviour or the conducting of an activity' (The Oxford English Dictionary).

Ethics is therefore concerned with

- Morality – the difference between right and wrong – 'doing the right thing'.
- How one should act in a certain situation.

Business ethics is simply the application of ethical principles to the problems typically encountered in a business setting.

What influences our ethical viewpoint?

Why should we bother with Ethics?

Possible advantages	Possible disadvantages
• To protect the public interest • To avoid discipline/fines • Improved reputation • Good ethics can attract customers • Good ethics can result in a more effective workforce • Ethics can give cost savings • Ethics can reduce risk	• Increased cost of sourcing materials from ethical sources • Lose profit by not trading with unethical customers/suppliers • Waste of management time?

Fundamental Principles (IFAC Code of Ethics)

The main advantages of a principles-based approach over a rules-based approach are that a principles-based approach is applicable to all situations, and gives individuals less chance of finding loopholes.

Integrity

- A professional accountant should be straightforward and honest in all professional and business relationships.
- Integrity also implies fair dealing and truthfulness.

Objectivity

- A professional accountant should not allow bias, conflict of interest or undue influence of others to override professional or business judgments.
- Need independence of mind and of appearance.

Professional competence

- A professional accountant has a continuing duty to maintain professional knowledge and skill at the level required to ensure that a client or employer receives competent professional service based on current developments in practice, legislation and techniques.
- A professional accountant should act diligently and in accordance with applicable technical and professional standards when providing professional services.

Confidentiality

- A professional accountant should respect the confidentiality of information acquired as a result of professional and business relationships and should not disclose any such information to third parties without proper and specific authority unless there is a legal or professional right or duty to disclose.

- Confidential information acquired as a result of professional and business relationships should not be used for the personal advantage of the professional accountant or third parties.

Professional behaviour

- A professional accountant should comply with relevant laws and regulations and should avoid any action that discredits the profession.

Threats

The self-interest threat

- May occur due to financial or other self-interest conflict

- e.g. fear of losing a client if you don't do what they ask.

The self-review threat

- May occur when previous judgement needs to be re-evaluated by the member responsible for that judgement

- e.g. doing accounts and then auditing them – would you admit to errors?

The advocacy threat

- May occur when a member promotes a position or opinion to the point that subsequent objectivity may be compromised

- e.g. arguing strongly with the tax office to try and reduce a client's tax bill – are you still being fair and truthful?

The familiarity or trust threat

- May occur when, because of a close or personal relationship, a member becomes too sympathetic to the interests of others
- e.g. having audited a client for 20 years do you fail to do enough testing as you trust them that the accounts are OK?

The intimidation threat

- May occur when a member may be deterred from acting objectively by threats, whether real or perceived
- e.g. Your employer or client may be very dominating or threatening so you just do whatever they say.

Safeguards

Safeguards are controls that mitigate, reduce or eliminate ethical threats

Two types:

- Safeguards created by the profession, legislation or regulation
  - e.g. CPD requirements, passing exams.
- Safeguards in the work environment.
  - e.g. policies dealing with receiving gifts, ethics policy, whistle blowing.

Businesses often incorporate the International Federation of Accountants (IFAC) principles into their own formal ethical codes.

Money laundering

- Money laundering offences.
- Dealing with suspected money laundering.
- Tipping off.
- Customer due diligence.
- Whistleblowing.

Definition

Money laundering is the process of exchanging criminally obtained money or other assets for clean money or other assets with no obvious link to the criminal origins. It is also the term for any money used to fund terrorism activities.

Money laundering involves 3 main stages:

1. Placement – where cash obtained through criminal activity is first placed into the financial system.

2. Layering – where the illegal cash is disguised by passing it through complex transactions making it difficult to trace.

3. Integration – where the illegally obtained funds are moved back into the legitimate economy and is now 'clean'.

Terrorist financing is fund raising, possessing or dealing with property or facilitating someone else to do so, when intending, knowing or suspecting or having reasonable cause to suspect that it is intended for the purposes of terrorism.

Terrorist property is money or property likely to be used for terrorist purposes or the proceeds of commissioning or carrying out terrorist acts.

Conviction of money laundering or terrorist financing is punishable by up to **14 years** imprisonment and/or an unlimited fine.

Money laundering offences

- Acquiring, possession or use of criminal property.
- Concealing or disguising or transferring criminal property, or removing it from the country.
- Failure to disclose knowledge or suspicion of money laundering (see next page for more details).
- Tipping off (see later for more details).

Failure to report knowledge or suspicion of money laundering

- Failure by an individual in the regulated sector to inform the Financial Intelligence Unit (FIU) or the firm's Money Laundering Reporting Officer (MLRO), as soon as practicable, of knowledge or suspicion that another person is engaged in money laundering, or

- Failure by MLROs in the regulated sector to make the required report to the FIU as soon as practicable if an internal report leads them to know or suspect that a person is engaged in money laundering.

If a member does not report known or suspected money laundering they can be charged with the offence of 'failure to report'. Confidentiality is not a defence.

If a business fails to meet its obligations under the Regulations, civil penalties or criminal sanctions can be imposed on the business and any individuals deemed responsible. This could include anyone in a senior position who neglected their own responsibilities or agreed to something that resulted in the compliance failure.

Dealing with suspected money laundering

Businesses, which are designed to assist in detecting money laundering and preventing the financial services organisations being used for money laundering purposes.

De minimis exceptions are **not** available in relation to either money laundering or terrorist financing offences – no amount is too trivial not to bother about.

At a minimum, an anti-money laundering program should incorporate:

- Money laundering and terrorist financing risk assessment.

- Implementation of systems, policies, controls and procedures that effectively manage the risk that the firm is exposed to in relation to money laundering activities and ensure compliance with the legislation, including:

  - Appointment of a Money Laundering Reporting Officer (MLRO).

  - Establishing internal reporting procedures to the MLRO.

  - Procedures for the reporting of suspicious transactions to the Financial Intelligence Unit (FIU).

  - Communication and training of all staff in the main requirements of the legislation.

  - Independent audit function to assess adequacy and effectiveness of the firm's procedures.

- Compliance with customer due diligence, enhanced due diligence and simplified due diligence requirements.

- Enhanced record keeping and data protection systems, policies and procedures.

Procedure for reporting known or suspected money laundering

There is no formal definition of suspicious. A suspicious transaction will often be inconsistent with the client's known or usual legitimate activities. Examples include:

- Unusually large cash deposits.
- Frequent exchanges of cash into other currencies.
- Overseas business arrangements with no clear business purpose.

It is a criminal offence not to report knowledge or suspicion of money laundering. Money laundering regulations require that:

- A person in the organisation is nominated to receive disclosures (usually an MLRO).
- Anyone in the organisation who suspects that a person is engaged in money laundering must disclose it to the MLRO.
- Where a disclosure is made to the MLRO, they must consider it in the light of any relevant information which is available to the organisation and determine whether it gives rise to suspicion.

- Where the MLRO does suspect money laundering, the information must be disclosed in a Suspicious Activity Report (SAR) to a regulatory body authorised for the purposes of these regulations (the FIU), such as the NCA in the UK.
- A SAR identifies:
    - Suspect's name, address, date of birth and nationality
    - Any identification or references seen
    - Nature of the activities giving rise to suspicion
    - Any other information that may be relevant i.e. the location of the laundered property, information held by the individual which identifies other parties involved in or connected to the matter.
- If there is no MLRO within the organisation then the SAR goes directly to the FIU (NCA in the UK).

Tipping off

Tipping off is telling the money laundering offender that the authorities have been informed or disclosing anything that might prejudice an investigation.

The penalty for this offence is a maximum of **two years** imprisonment, or an unlimited fine, or both.

A tipping off disclosure may be made in writing or verbally, and either directly or indirectly.

Customer due diligence

When considering any new client engagement, the professional accountant should assess the likelihood of money laundering.

Money Laundering Regulations 2017

Money laundering regulations state that Customer Due Diligence (CDD) must be applied in the following situations:

- When establishing a new business relationship.
- When carrying out an occasional transaction (i.e. involving £8,361, or the equivalent in Euros, or more).
- Where there is a suspicion of money laundering or terrorist financing.
- Where there are doubts about previously obtained customer identification information.
- At appropriate times, to existing clients, on a risk-sensitive basis.

If an organisation has a turnover of less than £100,000 (or the equivalent in Euros) they may be exempt as there is little risk of money laundering activity and to comply with the regulations would be an unnecessary burden.

When to apply Customer Due Diligence (CDD)

CDD must be performed as soon as reasonably practical after contact is first made between the two parties. Where satisfactory evidence of identity is not obtained by the accountant, the business relationship or occasional transaction must not proceed any further.

Whistleblowing

Whistleblowing means disclosing information that a worker believes is evidence of illegality, gross waste, gross mismanagement, abuse of power, or substantial and specific danger to the public health and safety.

Many organisations (e.g. the NHS) have policies and procedures for 'internal' whistle blowing.

'External' whistle blowing could involve, for example, going to newspapers.

In the UK the Public Interest Disclosure Act 1998 protects you from dismissal by your employer provided you are acting in good faith.

12

Technology affecting business and finance

- Offshoring/outsourcing.
- Cloud computing.
- Cloud accounting.
- The impact of emerging and developing technologies on accounting systems.

Repetitive tasks (for example, associated with the financial close and regulatory reporting and account reconciliation) are most likely to be automated, but developments in technology are allowing more **complex tasks** to be automated also.

Advantages

- Cost savings
- Focus on value adding activities
- Improved accuracy
- Positive return on investment
- Adaptability

Disadvantages

- Job/role uncertainty
- Relationship management
- IT staff competence required
- Training
- Change management

Finance professionals should not view automation as a threat but as an opportunity.

AI and machine learning

Artificial Intelligence is a system's ability to correctly interpret external data, to learn from such data, and to use those learnings to achieve specific goals and tasks through flexible adaptation.

This is often considered in the context of human-type robotics but reaches much further than this, and is set to transform the way we live and work.

Some of the more advanced activities and skills artificial intelligence can now master, and therefore present huge opportunities for developers and companies alike, include:

- Voice recognition
- Planning
- Learning
- Problem solving

Blockchain

A blockchain is a decentralised, distributed and public digital ledger that is used to record transactions across many computers. This means the record cannot be altered retroactively without the alteration of all subsequent blocks and the consensus of the network.

Key features of a blockchain:

- In a blockchain system, transactions are recorded by a number of participants using a network which operates via the internet.

- When a transaction takes place (for example, between a buyer and a seller) the details of that deal are recorded by everyone.

- The process of verifying the transaction is carried out by computers. This decentralised network of computers ensures that a single system cannot add new blocks to the chain.

- When a new block is added to a blockchain, it is linked to the previous block using a cryptographic hash (this turns data into a format that can only be read by authorised users) generated from the contents of the previous block.

- Blockchains and accounting.

- Ultimately, blockchain provides an unalterable, transparent record of all accountancy-related data.

- Examples of how blockchain can benefit the accounting profession include:

- Reducing the cost and of maintaining and reconciling ledgers.

- Providing absolute certainty over the ownership and history of assets, the existence of obligations and the measurement of amounts owed to a business and owed by a business.

- Freeing up time to allow staff to concentrate on other responsibilities such as planning, valuation, reporting etc., rather than record-keeping.

Electronic filing of documents

An electronic file management system is a good option for a variety of businesses across a number of different industries. Government agencies, medical practices, insurance companies, legal firms, finance functions and highly technical industries may all benefit from an electronic file management system.

Documentation previously stored on paper (or some physical format), becomes more valuable and easier to use when translated into an electronic format.

Benefits

- Reliable backup assistance and disaster recovery methods.

- Accurate, organised electronic databases.

- Instant, 24/7 access, no matter where the user is located.

- Increased workplace productivity.

- Enhanced customer service.

Disadvantages

- A sizeable initial set up cost for the system.

- The need to keep hardware and software up to date.

- Data security and the risk of data breaches.

Electronic signing of documents

Electronic signatures deliver a way to sign documents in the online world, much like one signs a document with a pen in the offline world.

Electronic signatures come in many forms, including:

- Typewritten.

- Scanned.

- An electronic representation of a handwritten signature.

- A unique representation of characters.

- A digital representation of characteristics, for example, fingerprint or retina scan.

- A signature created by cryptographic means.

Data analytics

Data analytics is the process of collecting, organising and analysing large sets of data (big data) to discover patterns and other information which an organisation can use to inform future decisions.

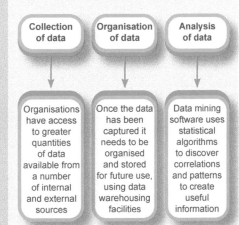

Collection of data	Organisation of data	Analysis of data
Organisations have access to greater quantities of data available from a number of internal and external sources	Once the data has been captured it needs to be organised and stored for future use, using data warehousing facilities	Data mining software uses statistical algorithms to discover correlations and patterns to create useful information

Benefits

- Fresh insight and understanding
- Performance improvement
- Market segmentation and customisation
- Decision making
- Innovation
- Risk management

Offshoring/outsourcing

Definition

Offshoring refers to the process of outsourcing or relocating some of an organisation's functions from one country to another, usually in an effort to reduce costs.

Offshoring would not have been possible without the improvements in technology that allowed seamless communication between customers and business functions in locations across the world.

Benefits of offshoring:

- Cost savings

Disadvantages of offshoring:

- Cultural differences and language barriers

Outsourcing

Definition

Outsourcing means contracting out aspects of the work of the organisation previously done in-house, to specialist providers.

An organisation will often outsource its non-core services to a third party, allowing them to focus on their core competencies which are integral to the organisation's ability to create and to add value.

Benefits of outsourcing:

- Staff are freed up to focus on value adding activities to gain competitive advantage.

- The cost structure of the business will change, allowing cost savings to be achieved.

- Improved productivity as the outsourced work is now being done by experts who may also use automation.

- Supplier expertise can also lead to improved accuracy and adherence to regulations.

Disadvantages of outsourcing:

- Cost issues – the supplier will want to make a profit margin.

- Loss of core competence.

- Transaction costs.

- Finality of decision.

- Risk of loss of confidential information.

- Risk of continuity of supply if the supplier has problems.

- Difficulty agreeing/enforcing contract terms.

- Damage to employee morale if redundancies occur or if organisational culture is eroded.

Cloud computing

Definition

Cloud computing is the delivery of on-demand computing resources – everything from applications to data centres – over the internet. (IBM).

The basic idea and application of cloud computing sees users log in to an account in order to access, manage and process files and software via remote servers hosted on the internet. This replaces the traditional method of owning and running software locally on a computer or networked server.

Advantages

- Flexibility and scalability
- Cost efficient
- Security
- Flexible working
- Environment

Disadvantages

- Organisational change
- Contract management
- Security, privacy and compliance
- Reliance

Cloud accounting

Definition

Cloud accounting is a system whereby users subscribe to an online accounting software solution and move their books to the cloud. Cloud accounting software holds accounts data remotely on secure servers (not onsite on the company's computers).

Benefits

- Access to real-time financial performance and position information.
- Multi-user access for online collaboration: cloud accounting enables access to large networks.
- Nothing to install or update, automatic backup.
- More apps and plug-ins are available.
- Access levels can be controlled.
- Security and privacy should be airtight.
- Access from any location with an internet connection.
- Software updates delivered faster and more easily by cloud provider.

Disadvantages

- Users' ability to connect depends on internet connection.
- Supplier's ability to adhere to data protection regulations will be crucial.
- May become difficult to switch providers/ systems.

The impact of emerging and developing technologies on accounting systems

- Process automation and the use of AI and machine learning can provide opportunities for finance teams to automate repetitive work and concentrate on adding value to the business.

- The use of blockchain technology along with electronic filing and signing can add security and integrity to transactions and documents.

Offshoring/outsourcing

- Technological advantages have made these possible.

- The use of offshoring and outsourcing leads to changes in a business's cost structure, allows it to access new markets and to operate from anywhere.

Cloud accounting

- Cloud computing involves accessing software and data over the internet rather than from an office based server.

- Cloud accounting offers flexibility but businesses must be aware of its risks.

chapter 13

Data protection, information security and cybersecurity

- GDPR.
- Cybersecurity.

GDPR

Legislation which details the following principles about data:

- Used fairly, lawfully and transparently.
- Used for specified, explicit purposes (Purpose limitation).
- Used in a way that is adequate, relevant and limited to only what is necessary.
- Accurate and, where required, kept up to date.
- Kept for no longer than is necessary (storage limitation).
- Handled in a way that ensures appropriate security.
- Accountability – ability to prove that the regulations are being complied with.

Data protection breaches

As the business world becomes more complex, organisations are holding increasing amounts of data about individuals.

Data protection is concerned with protecting individuals against the misuse of this information.

If an organisation fails to comply with the GDPR, it can be fined.

EU maximum fines – the higher of €20 million or 4% of annual global turnover.

UK maximum fines – the higher of £17.5 million or 4% of annual global turnover.

Requirements:

- Report a breach to the relevant supervisory authority within 72 hours of becoming aware of the breach, where feasible.
- If the breach is likely to result in a high risk of adversely affecting individuals' rights and freedoms, the organisation

must also inform those individuals without undue delay.

- Organisations should ensure that they have robust breach detection, investigation and internal reporting procedures in place, in order to facilitate decision-making about whether or not there is a need to notify the relevant supervisory authority or the affected individuals, or both.

- Records must be kept of any personal data breaches, regardless of whether notification to the authorities or the individuals concerned is required.

Cybersecurity

Definition

Cyber security is the protection of internet-connected systems, including hardware, software and data, from cyber attacks.

A **cyber attack** is a malicious and deliberate attempt by an individual or organisation to breach the information system of another individual or organisation.

Key risks of cyber attacks

Risk	Description
Malware	Software designed to cause damage to a single computer, server or computer network. Worms, viruses and trojans are all varieties of malware, distinguished from one another by the means by which they reproduce and spread. These attacks may render a computer or network inoperable, or grant the attacker access so that they can control the system remotely.
Phishing	Cybercriminals craft emails to fool a target into taking some harmful action. The recipient might be tricked into downloading malware that is disguised as an important document or urged to click on a link that takes them to a fake website where they will be asked for sensitive information like usernames and password.
Denial of service	A brute force method to try to stop an online service from working properly.
Man in the middle	Attackers manage to interpose themselves secretly between the user and a web service that they are trying to access.

14

Information and Big Data

- Information.
- Big Data.

Information

Definition

Data consists of numbers, letters, symbols, raw facts, events and transactions which have been recorded but not yet processed into a form that is suitable for making decisions.

Information is data that has been processed in such a way that is has a meaning to the person that receives it, who may then use it to improve the quality of decision-making.

Information is a vital requirement within any business and is required both internally and externally.

Characteristics of good information

Good information should be:

Accurate

Complete

Cost effective

Understandable

Relevant

Authoritative

Timely

Easy to use

Big data

Big Data is a term for a collection of data which is so large it becomes difficult to store and process using traditional databases and data processing applications.

The five V's: represent the defining characteristics of Big Data:

- **Velocity**: Data is now streaming from sources such as social media sites at a virtually constant rate and current processing servers are unable to cope with this flow and generate meaningful real-time analysis.

- **Volume**: More sources of data and an increase in data generation in the digital age combine to increase the volume of data to a potentially unmanageable level.

- **Variety**: Traditionally data was structured and in similar and consistent formats such as Excel spreadsheets and standard databases. Data can now be generated and collected in a huge range of formats including rich text, audio and GPS data amongst others.

- **Veracity**: Because of so many different sources there is an increased risk of inaccuracies.

- **Value**: Once businesses have the data it needs to be used in a way that adds value.

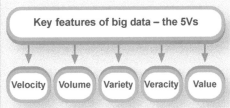

Key features of big data – the 5Vs

Velocity | Volume | Variety | Veracity | Value

Benefits of Big Data	Risks associated with Big Data
• Drives innovation – can be used to develop the next generation of products or services • Improves customer service and decision making • Can create new revenue streams • Source of competitive advantage • Ensures measurable outcomes	• Skills to use systems may not exist • Security of data • Valuable time may be spent measuring relationships that have no organisational value • Incorrect data may result in incorrect conclusions • Technical difficulties integrating systems • Cost of establishing hardware and software

Big Data analytics

Big Data analytics is the process of scrutinising Big Data to identify patterns, correlations, relationships and other insights. This information can inform decision making and have a wide reaching effect on the organisation's competitive strategy and marketing campaigns. It can therefore have a direct impact on future profitability.

15

Visualising information

- – Methods of communication.
- – Good communication.
- – Using tables.
- – Using images.
- – Using IT.

Methods of communicating
- Report
- Note
- Letter
- Memorandum
- Email

Good communication
- Use the house style
- Consider confidentiality
- Choose the best format

Visualising information

Using tables
- Simple tables
- Matrices

Using images
- Bar charts
- Pie charts
- Graphs
- Area graphs

Using IT
- Dashboards
- Dealing with outliers

Index

A

Artificial Intelligence 90

B

Barriers to entry 67
Big Data 105
Big Data analytics 106
Blockchain 91
Blockchain technology 98

C

Chairman 18
Characteristics of good information 104
Charities 12
Cloud accounting 97, 98
Cloud computing 96
Clubs 7
Commercial companies 7
Companies House 17
Competition 66
Confidentiality 78
Conflicts 27
Connected 24, 26
Cooperatives 7

Corporate social responsibility 72
CSR 72
Customer due diligence 86, 87
Cyber attack 101
Cyber security 101

D

Data 104
Data analytics 93
Data protection breaches 100
Debt 13
Denial of service 102
Directors 16, 18
Directors duties 19

E

Electronic filing of documents 92
Electronic signing of documents 93
Entrepreneurial 32
Equilibrium 65
Equity 13
Ethics 77
Executive director 18
External 24, 26

F

Fair value 21
Financial Conduct Authority (FCA) 17
Firm 20

G

GDPR 100
General partnership 20
Goodwill 21

I

IFAC code of ethics 78
Information 104
Integration 82
Integrity 78
Internal 24, 26

J

Joint and several 21

L

Layering 82
Limited liability companies 8

M

Malware 102
Managing director 18
Man in the middle 102
Mendelow's 28
Money laundering 81, 82
Money laundering offences 83
Monopolistic competition 66
Monopoly 66

N

Non-executive director 18
Not-for-profit 7
Not-for-profit organisations (NFPs) 7, 9

O

Objectivity 78
Offshoring 94
Oligopoly 66
Organisational types 7
Organisations 6
Outsourcing 95
Ownership/control 7

P

Partnership 20
Partnerships 7
People 71
Phishing 102
Placement 82
Planet 71
Primary 24
Private sector 7, 10, 12
Private sector limited liability 7
Process automation 98
Professional behaviour 79
Professional competence 78
Profit 5, 9, 15, 17, 71
Profit orientation 7
Profit-seeking 7
Public sector 7, 10

R

Repetitive tasks 90
Risk averse 24
Risk neutral 24
Risk seeking 24
Robotics 90

S

Safeguards 80
Secondary 24
Separation of ownership and control 12
Services vs. manufacuring organisations 11
Shareholders 16, 20, 70
Shifts in supply 65
Social needs 7
Sole traders 8
Stakeholders 25
Sustainability 69

T

TBL 72, 73
The advocacy threat 79
The familiarity or trust threat 80
The intimidation threat 80
The price mechanism 65
The self-interest threat 79
The self-review threat 79
Threats 79
Tipping off 86
Triple bottom line reporting 72
Types of funding 12

U

Unlimited liability partnerships 16, 20

V

Variety 105
Velocity 105
Veracity 105
Visualising information 108
Volume 105

W

Whistleblowing 87